Who Was
Laura Ingalls Wilder?

Who Was
Laura Ingalls Wilder?

by Patricia Brennan Demuth

illustrated by Tim Foley

Grosset & Dunlap
An Imprint of Penguin Random House

For Maya Demuth, born at home
on a mountain in Maui—PBD

For my father, on his epic journey these past six months—TF

GROSSET & DUNLAP
Penguin Young Readers Group
An Imprint of Penguin Random House LLC

Text copyright © 2013 by Patricia Brennan. Illustrations copyright © 2013 by Tim Foley. Cover illustration copyright © 2013 by Penguin Random House LLC. All rights reserved. Published by Grosset & Dunlap, an imprint of Penguin Random House LLC, 345 Hudson Street, New York, New York 10014. Who HQ™ and all related logos are trademarks owned by Penguin Random House LLC. GROSSET & DUNLAP is a trademark of Penguin Random House LLC. Printed in the USA.

Library of Congress Control Number: 2013032701

ISBN 978-0-448-46706-1   10 9

Contents

Who Was
Laura Ingalls Wilder?

In 1874, two horses slowly pulled a covered wagon across the open prairie. The man with the reins, Charles Ingalls, had twinkly blue eyes and a long curly beard. Inside the wagon were his wife and daughters, plus everything the family owned.

A seven-year-old girl named Laura gazed out the back of the wagon. She saw an enormous green prairie stretching to the skyline. Not a tree was in sight. How different this was from the woodland home she had left behind in Wisconsin.

The Ingallses were traveling west. They didn't know exactly where they would end up. This wasn't the first time they had moved to a new home by covered wagon. And it wouldn't be the last. They were part of a huge wave of pioneers pouring out of the East to settle the vast stretches of untamed land in the middle of America.

To young Laura, this trip meant adventure. At nights, the family camped outside and Pa played his fiddle. Laura thought that "the stars were singing."

The Ingallses would enjoy many happy times like this. But they faced terrible hardships, too. Everything about frontier life was extreme. In winter, there were blizzards. In summer, the land was sometimes as dry as dust. There was sickness and the danger of wild animals. The Ingallses would need to draw on deep wells of courage in order to survive.

Even after Laura's childhood was long past, her memories remained strong. In her sixties, Laura started to write a book for children called *Little House in the Big Woods*. Laura kept writing until she had a whole series of books about her childhood.

Laura's pa liked to call her "little half-pint" and "flutterbudget." But the world came to know her as Laura Ingalls Wilder, one of the best-loved children's authors ever.

Chapter 1
Wagon Trail

Laura Ingalls was born a pioneer. Her parents were pioneers, and so were her grandparents. She was born on February 7, 1867, in a log cabin that Pa built. The place was Pepin, Wisconsin, in an area known as the "Big Woods."

Pa (Charles Ingalls) grew up in New York
State. Cities in the East were growing bigger and
bigger. New York City already teemed with over
three hundred thousand people. That life wasn't
right for the Ingalls family. They wanted land
of their own on the wide-open frontier. So they
moved west. In time they settled in Wisconsin,
near the farm where Ma (Caroline Quiner) grew
up. Ma's family had come from Connecticut.

But pioneer spirit had driven them west, too.
The Ingallses and Quiners were good neighbors.
They got along so well that three of the Ingallses
married three of the Quiners!

Ma was a schoolteacher before she married Pa. Calm and gentle, she loved Pa's bright personality. Pa played the fiddle, worked hard, and dreamed big dreams.

By the time Laura was two, Wisconsin was getting too crowded for Pa. The edge of the frontier had moved west of the Mississippi, and Pa wanted to move with it. He and Ma decided to go to Kansas.

For several weeks, the Ingallses traveled in a covered wagon. There were no roads, just wagon trails. Rivers and streams had to be forded.

PRAIRIE SCHOONERS

LIKE MOST PIONEERS, THE INGALLSES
TRAVELED IN A COVERED WAGON. IT WAS KNOWN
AS A PRAIRIE SCHOONER. A SCHOONER IS A BOAT.
AND THE CLOTH COVER ON THE WAGON LOOKED
SOMETHING LIKE A SAIL. SIX OR SEVEN ARCHED
TREE BOWS, ATTACHED TO THE SIDES OF THE
WAGON, HELD UP THE CANVAS TOP. THE WHEELS
WERE MADE OF WOOD AND RIMMED WITH
IRON. THE BED OF THE WAGON WAS MADE AS
WATERTIGHT AS POSSIBLE SO IT COULD FLOAT
ACROSS RIVERS AND STREAMS.

Sometimes Pa jumped into the water to calm the horses. It must have been a long, bumpy trip for little Laura and her four-year-old sister, Mary.

Somewhere near the Kansas border, the wagon tracks ended. It seemed a good place to stop. It wasn't! The Ingallses were in Indian Territory on land that still belonged to the Osage tribe. Pa thought it was okay for pioneers to settle there. But he was wrong.

Pa built the family another log cabin. Few
trees grew on the flat, grassy plains of Kansas, so
logs came from trees that grew at a nearby creek.
Laura's earliest memories were of the time she
spent in this house.

One night Pa carried Laura to the window to
see a pack of howling wolves. They surrounded
the house, with their faces pointing to the moon.
In *Little House on the Prairie,* Laura wrote that
their "eyes glittered green" and "their howls
shuddered through the house."

Laura always remembered this night with awe. Nature filled her with wonder. And as long as she was with her family, she felt safe and secure.

On the prairie, danger was never far away. Laura's whole family fell deathly ill with malaria. A doctor named George Tann gave them a bitter medicine called quinine. Dr. Tann was an African American. Few African Americans lived on the frontier. Luckily for the Ingallses, Dr. Tann was there to save their lives.

In the spring of 1870, tensions grew between the Osages and the settlers. The US government wanted to push the Osages farther west—to Oklahoma. The Osages held councils. Would they stay and fight, or leave? Night after night, the Ingallses heard their loud cries and wild drum-beating. In the end, the Osages decided to leave peacefully. They knew they were vastly outnumbered by the settlers who wanted their land.

OSAGE NATION

BEFORE SETTLERS CAME, THE OSAGES LIVED
IN A VAST AREA OF THE OHIO RIVER VALLEY.
GRADUALLY THEY LOST THEIR LANDS IN TREATIES

WITH THE US GOVERNMENT. BY THE TIME THE
INGALLSES ARRIVED, THE OSAGES WERE LIVING
IN A FIFTY-MILE-WIDE RESERVATION IN KANSAS.
THE OSAGES HAD TO GIVE UP EVEN THAT LAND
IN A TREATY IN 1870. THE NATION SETTLED ON
A RESERVATION IN WHAT IS NOW OKLAHOMA,
WHERE THEY LIVE TODAY.

THE OSAGES WERE BIG-GAME HUNTERS. TWICE
A YEAR, THE ENTIRE TRIBE LEFT THEIR VILLAGES
AND HUNTED BUFFALO ON THE PLAINS. MEN OF THE
TRIBE WERE WELL-KNOWN FOR
THEIR HEIGHT, USUALLY
STANDING OVER SIX
FEET TALL. THEY
SHAVED THEIR HEADS
EXCEPT FOR A LOCK
OF HAIR ON TOP. ALL
OF THE OSAGES WORE
BEAUTIFUL CLOTHING—
SOFT DEER AND
BUFFALO SKINS
DECORATED WITH
BEADS AND FEATHERS.

Young Laura did not understand what was happening to the Osage people. But she remembered seeing them ride past the Ingallses' cabin in a long, sad line.

Shortly afterward, the Ingallses left Kansas, too. The man who had bought the Ingallses' cabin in Wisconsin couldn't afford to keep it. He wanted the Ingallses to take back their farm. So the family returned to Laura's birthplace in the Big Woods.

Laura was four when they left their little house on the prairie. But the prairie would call the Ingallses back again.

Chapter 2
The Big Woods

Back in Wisconsin, Laura looked forward to a treat that came just once a year: roasted pig tail! In the fall, the Ingallses roasted the family pig to have meat for the winter. The pig had roamed wild all year. Besides eating the tail, the kids got to play with a balloon made from the blown-up pig bladder!

In the Big Woods, Pa hunted for rabbit, squirrels, deer, and bears.

He made bullets by pouring melted lead into
a mold. Ma cooked what Pa brought home in
big pots on the woodstove. Pa trapped, too—for
mink, foxes, and wolves that he sold in town. Ma
churned cream into golden lumps of butter. The
secret for making it yellow was scraping in carrots.
Pa built all the furniture—tables, chairs, and
beds. Ma sewed all the clothes.

She sewed Laura a rag doll, too, painting on the smile with ink made from pokeberries.

In the winter of 1873, when Laura was six, Pa's "itchy foot" acted up again. That was what he called his restless spirit. This time he wanted to move to open grasslands in western Minnesota. The railroad went there now. New towns were springing up along the tracks.

Winter was a good time to go because the Mississippi River was frozen. The Ingallses could drive their wagon straight across the ice. But the girls came down with scarlet fever. By the time they were well enough to travel, the ice was much thinner.

Laura never forgot the sounds of the creaking ice as the family crossed the Mississippi. It was terrifying! That night, the family heard sharp exploding sounds. The ice was splitting apart. They had made it across just in time!

"All's well that ends well," said Pa. It became
one of Laura's favorite sayings.

On the other side of the river, the family found
a cabin to stay in until spring. Then they set out
on the trail again. Everywhere Laura looked was a
sea of rippling grasses.

During stops, Laura ran free in the tall grass.
Her sunbonnet dangled down her back. The
warm sunshine on her face felt wonderful. Mary
kept her sunbonnet tied under her chin, like
Ma wanted. Ma was teaching her girls to be
ladylike—even on the trail. Being quiet and good
seemed easy for Mary. But not for an active girl
like Laura.

The Ingallses' wagon stopped in Walnut Grove, Minnesota. Pa bought a farm "on the banks of Plum Creek." That would later be the title of one of Laura's books.

The farm came with a house—a very unusual house. It looked like a cave dug into the bank of the creek. The front was made of sod bricks. Thick roots of prairie grasses held the bricks together.

At first Laura wasn't sure she liked living in a dugout. Everything was made of dirt—the floor, ceiling, and walls. Snakes and bugs might crawl out of the walls! Grass grew on the roof because the roof was part of the plains. One time the

family ox ran over the roof and rammed its leg straight through!

Soon enough, Laura didn't mind the dugout. She was learning the pioneer way of "making do." And anyway, Pa was building a new house with store-bought boards and windows!

SOD HOUSES

THE PLAINS WERE ALMOST TREELESS. SO SETTLERS MADE SOD HOUSES BY CUTTING "BRICKS" OUT OF THE GRASS-COVERED GROUND. THEN THEY LAID THE BRICKS ROOT-SIDE UP SO THE BRICKS COULD GROW INTO ONE ANOTHER. OVER TIME, SOD WALLS BECAME VERY STRONG AND SOLID.

ALTHOUGH SOD HOMES WERE SMALL AND DARK, THEY OFFERED GOOD PROTECTION AGAINST BOTH COLD AND HEAT. ALSO, THEY WERE FIREPROOF, KEEPING DWELLERS SAFE FROM FIERCE PRAIRIE FIRES.

A STANDARD SOD HOUSE WAS FREESTANDING. SOME SETTLERS MADE DUGOUTS INSTEAD, BY TUNNELING INTO THE SIDE OF A HILL AND BUILDING A SOD WALL IN FRONT.

Chapter 3
School Days

Mary and Laura started school in Walnut
Grove. The schoolhouse had just one room
and one teacher for all grades. There was one
blackboard—an actual board painted black.

School was two and a half miles from home,
and the girls walked the whole way.

Seven-year-old Laura was very shy at first.
She wasn't used to other children. But Laura was
spunky. Before long, she was leading the girls in
games at recess.

One classmate named Nellie Owens made fun of Laura and Mary for being farm girls. Nellie's father owned a store in town. She had pretty clothes and new toys. Nellie's teasing made Laura mad.

In the Little House books, Laura turned Nellie into a character named Nellie Oleson. Then millions of readers disliked Nellie as much as Laura did.

At home, Laura was happy. Every morning, she got up before sunrise to walk the cow to pasture. Rising at dawn became a lifelong habit.

Besides caring for the cow, her other chores were sewing, gardening, cooking, and watching over Carrie, her little sister who had been born in Kansas.

Then disaster flew in on the wind.

Just before the harvest of 1875, the Ingallses watched an odd dark cloud appear in the sky.

Suddenly, Laura felt things hailing down on her.
Grasshoppers! Millions of them! They fell to earth

and started eating everything that grew. Soon the
prairie was covered inches thick with insects.

GRASSHOPPER SWARMS

NORMALLY A GRASSHOPPER LIVES ALONE. BUT WHEN IT'S VERY DRY AND HOT, GRASSHOPPERS SOMETIMES JOIN TOGETHER IN GIANT SWARMS THAT ARE CARRIED BY THE WIND. FOR FIVE YEARS, FROM 1873 TO 1877, GRASSHOPPER SWARMS DESTROYED CROPS IN

WESTERN MINNESOTA. THEY APPEARED IN CLOUDS
THAT WERE OVER 275 MILES WIDE. THE THICK
SWARMS BLOCKED OUT THE SUN. BESIDES
DEVOURING ALL THAT GREW, THE HUNGRY INSECTS
ATE WOOL FROM LIVE SHEEP AND CLOTHES OFF
PEOPLE'S BACKS. USUALLY A SWARM STAYED TWO
TO SEVEN DAYS IN ONE PLACE. THEN THEY LEFT
THE SAME WAY THEY CAME IN: ON THE WIND.

Pa tried desperately to save his wheat crop. He lit fires around the fields to smoke out the grasshoppers. But it was useless. In a few days, the green prairie had turned brown. The grasshoppers flew away on the wind. But Pa's wheat crop was wiped out.

What would the Ingallses do now?

Pa decided to go east until he came to a farm where grasshoppers hadn't destroyed the crops. He'd work to earn money and then return home. With no money for train fare, Pa ended up walking two hundred miles!

Happily, Pa returned with enough money to last the winter. Then a special surprise came. Laura's little brother, Freddy, was born.

The following spring, millions of grasshoppers hatched from eggs laid the year before. What was the sense of planting more wheat? It would just be destroyed. So when a friend of Pa's asked him to come to Iowa to help manage a hotel, Pa said yes.

The Ingallses sold their farm and new wooden house. Pa said no "pesky mess of grasshoppers" could beat them. But the hard times were not over.

On the way to Iowa, the Ingallses stopped by to see relatives in eastern Minnesota. While there, Laura's little brother suddenly took ill and died. Freddy was just nine months old.

Laura never wrote about her little brother. Losing him was too sad for her, and she thought it would be too sad for readers, as well.

Chapter 4
Coming and Going

Ma believed that "it takes all kinds of people to make a world." The truth of that saying became clear to Laura in her new Iowa home—which happened to be a big hotel!

The hotel in Burr Oak seemed grand to Laura.
There were eleven rooms and a wide front porch!
Ma and Pa both worked at the hotel. Ma did
laundry, cooking, and cleaning for the guests.
Laura and Mary also had jobs, washing dishes and
waiting on tables.

Next door was a saloon with a bullet hole in the door. A man who was drunk had shot at—and missed!—his wife. The exciting story gave Laura a thrill. But it did not please her parents, who wanted to keep their girls away from the rowdy barroom. Soon they moved

to a little house at the edge of town.

Burr Oak was an "old town." Unlike newer
frontier towns, many houses were made of brick.
So was the two-story school that Mary and Laura
attended.

There were fifty-seven kids in Laura's class! Laura shone in her studies. Not only bright, she worked hard to stay at the top. Reading books became one of her greatest pleasures. She'd get lost in them for hours.

One day Laura came home from school to find a woman talking to Ma. She wanted to adopt

Laura! Ma smiled. No, she said, she couldn't possibly do without Laura. In those days, families sometimes let a child be adopted, especially if times were tough. Laura knew her family would always stick together, no matter what.

Laura badly missed the prairie. She didn't like the dusty town. Neither did Pa and Ma. When word came that the grasshoppers had left Walnut Grove, the family packed up to return to Minnesota.

This time, there was another little girl in the wagon. Laura's baby sister, Grace, had been born in Iowa. Now the Ingalls family was complete. There was Pa and Ma and four daughters: Mary (thirteen), Laura (eleven), Carrie (seven), and baby Grace.

The girls in Walnut Grove were happy to see Laura. She became the leader once again. Mary was shocked by her sister playing ball games meant for boys, with hairpins tumbling from her hair.

The sisters were so different. Mary was well-behaved and quiet. Laura was high-spirited and strong-willed. Then a tragedy brought the girls closer than they had ever been.

One day a terrible headache and high fever
overcame Mary. She grew weaker and sicker.
Everyone, even the doctor, feared Mary would die.
Slowly, she got better—but Mary was left

blind. She "could not see even the brightest
light any more." Still, she stayed calm, never
complaining.

Mary's blindness greatly changed Laura's
life, too. Pa explained to Laura that from now
on she would need to be Mary's eyes. This new
role became very important to Laura. Whatever

Laura saw, she tried to help Mary "see," too. Laura trained herself to observe details and bring them alive in words. Mary said that Laura made pictures when she talked. Laura didn't know it, but she was preparing for her life as a writer.

The Ingallses were happy in Walnut Grove. But they didn't have a farm of their own anymore.

AUNT DOCIA

One day, Pa's sister, Aunt Docia, trotted into town. She had come by herself all the way from Wisconsin. And she had a special offer for Pa. Would he like to help her husband manage a railroad crew in Dakota Territory?

What an opportunity! Pa could save up money.

Then the Ingallses could put a claim on their own homestead! Pa itched to go. But would Ma agree? Yes, Ma said, on one condition: Dakota Territory would be their final move.

THE HOMESTEAD ACT

THE HOMESTEAD ACT OF 1862 PROMISED SETTLERS 160 ACRES—FOR FREE. IN RETURN, HOMESTEADERS HAD TO LIVE ON THE LAND FOR FIVE YEARS—THAT MEANT BUILDING A HOUSE, DIGGING A WELL, CLEARING UNBROKEN SOIL, AND PLANTING CROPS.

IN THE SECOND HALF OF THE 1800S, THE HOMESTEAD ACT SPURRED HUNDREDS OF THOUSANDS OF SETTLERS TO MOVE WEST. THEY CAME FROM THE EASTERN STATES AND ALSO FROM EUROPE. THEY PUT DOWN ROOTS, CLEARED LAND, AND BUILT TOWNS. BY 1900, HOMESTEADERS HAD LARGELY SETTLED THE GREAT PRAIRIES WEST OF THE MISSISSIPPI AND EAST OF THE ROCKY MOUNTAINS. THE FRONTIER WAS GONE.

Chapter 5
Dakota Territory

Laura looked outside the window at the prairie whizzing by. For the first time, Laura, her mother, and sisters were going west by train. The speed astonished Laura. In one morning, the train went as far as a horse could go in a week.

Somewhere in Minnesota, the train stopped.
Why? Because there were no more train tracks

ahead! Pa's railroad crew was laying the new track that would extend this line all the way through Dakota Territory, and beyond.

Pa had gone ahead of his family to start his new job. Now he met his wife and daughters at the station. They traveled the rest of the way to Dakota Territory by wagon.

Laura's new home was a railroad camp that sat all alone on the empty prairie. It looked like they were in the middle of nowhere. Ten years later, in 1889, it would become the state of South Dakota.

During the day, the air was filled with the loud clangs and bangs of railroad men driving spikes into the ground.

The railroad crews left for the winter, but not the Ingallses. Pa had agreed to watch the railroad company's equipment in exchange for staying in a two-story house. It was the biggest house that twelve-year-old Laura had ever lived in.

THE GREAT DAKOTA BOOM

THE GREAT DAKOTA BOOM REFERS TO THE HUNDREDS OF THOUSANDS OF PEOPLE WHO CAME TO LIVE IN DAKOTA TERRITORY BETWEEN 1878 AND 1887. THE ARRIVAL OF THE RAILROAD IN THE AREA CAUSED THE BOOM. TO ATTRACT SETTLERS, RAILROAD COMPANIES RAN ADS BOASTING ABOUT THE "BEST FARMING LANDS, BEST GRAZING LANDS IN THE WORLD!" ALMOST OVERNIGHT, PRAIRIE TOWNS GREW UP ALONG THE RAILROAD TRACKS, SPACED APART EVERY SEVEN TO TEN MILES.

By early spring, hopeful homesteaders started showing up—first in a trickle, then in a rush. The Great Dakota Boom had begun.

The Ingallses took in travelers who were heading west. Overnight their home turned into a boardinghouse. Men camped out on the floor, then left the next day.

Laura was Ma's oldest helper now. Together
they worked day and night—washing bedding,

cleaning, and cooking. Once, when Ma was sick in bed, Laura cooked for and fed the whole crowd by herself.

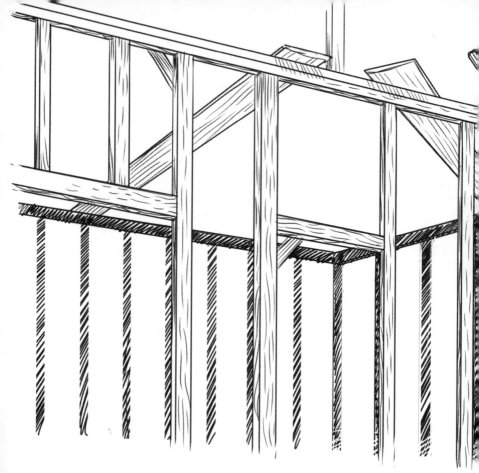

In February, Pa filed a claim for 160 acres in the town of De Smet. What town? Except for its name, the town didn't really exist. The location was near the railroad camp where the Ingallses had spent the winter. Pa also bought two lots in

town. He built a store on one lot and moved the
family there.

Laura had a close-up view of a town being born.
It was thrilling to see buildings sprout up in De
Smet. People were setting up shops along the new

Main Street. Soon De Smet had a hotel, bank, furniture store, school, drugstore, tailor shop, butcher shop, and blacksmith. Most of the stores sported fancy false fronts.

FALSE FRONTS

MOST STORES IN FRONTIER TOWNS HAD FALSE FRONTS TO ATTRACT CUSTOMERS. THEY WERE "TRYING TO MAKE BELIEVE THAT THE BUILDINGS WERE TWO STORIES HIGH," LAURA WROTE IN *LITTLE TOWN ON THE PRAIRIE*. THE BUILDING BEHIND A FALSE FRONT WAS JUST ONE STORY. USUALLY IT WAS PLAIN, MADE OF SOD OR LOGS. BUT THE FALSE FRONTS WERE MADE OF LUMBER WITH PHONY WINDOWS. THEY GAVE BOOMTOWNS A LOOK OF BEING MORE SETTLED AND PROSPEROUS.

Yet Laura was still a country girl at heart. She was glad when the family moved to the homestead. Pa first put up a shanty there, which he would add to later. It would be the fourth house he had made with his own hands.

Pa also built a stable, dug a well, broke the deeply rooted prairie sod, and planted wheat. Now

Laura was Pa's right arm. She never grew over five feet tall, but Laura was strong and determined to make life easier for her father.

The Ingallses had their homestead, and the future looked bright. But winter blizzards were on their way.

Chapter 6
A Hard Winter

The winter of 1880–1881 was one of the worst in Dakota history. The first blizzard howled across the prairie in October. The Ingallses quickly moved off the claim into town, where it was safer. But one blizzard followed another, burying De Smet in fifteen-foot drifts. The winter "did its best to blot out the town," Laura wrote. School closed for the season. And, with railroad tracks buried in snow, the trains stopped coming.

For six months, De Smet was cut off from the outside world. Before long, stores sold out of everything—flour, meat, wheat, and coal.

The Ingallses fought to survive. Laura wrote about "listening to the wind howl and shriek while the house rocked with the force of it." The bone-chilling cold sometimes dropped forty degrees below zero. The family huddled by the stove, but still their breath froze in the air.

When their coal supply was nearly gone, they
used the only fuel they had—hay! Laura helped Pa
twist and braid hay to make sticks that were tight
enough to burn slowly.

For food, the family ate potatoes and biscuits
made out of flour and water. When their flour
supply was gone, Ma ground wheat in a coffee
grinder. Then one day there was no more wheat,

either. The family, like others in town, was nearly starving.

Then two young men in town crossed the open prairie in a sleigh to get wheat from a homesteader. What they brought back saved the hungry townspeople.

One of the young heroes was named Almanzo Wilder. He would later play a very important part in Laura's life.

ALMANZO WILDER

Finally, spring returned—and so did the trains. Laura later looked back on what everyone called the Hard Winter. "It is times like this that test people," she said. If it was a test, Laura passed with flying colors.

The harsh winter drove some people back east. Still, De Smet kept growing by leaps and bounds. New board sidewalks were put down. A grain elevator was put up.

Now that Laura was fourteen, her old dislike of town life fell away. She felt a kinship with those who had suffered through the Hard Winter. And she took more interest in the strangers coming to live in De Smet.

School resumed. Pretty, lively, and generous, she was popular with both girls and boys. Laura

still stood out as a student. At night she would
read her lessons aloud so Mary could learn them,
too. She knew how hard it was for her sister to
miss out on school. At that time there was no
school for the blind in all of Dakota Territory.

Chapter 7
Growing Up

When Laura was fifteen, a surprise visitor came to the house. He was named Louis Bouchie. He lived twelve miles away in a small settlement that needed a schoolteacher. Word had gotten around that Laura was smart and capable. Would she like the job?

Not really! Mary had wanted to be a teacher. Laura never had. Then she found out she'd make forty dollars for the eight-week term. That was a fortune to Laura!

There was a school for the blind in Iowa. Pa and Ma had brought Mary there. This special school cost money, something the Ingallses never had a lot of. Laura's job meant she could help pay for Mary's schooling. Yes, agreed Laura. She'd take the job.

The challenge scared Laura, though. One day she was a student, the next day she had students of her own. And she was going to live with the Bouchies—total strangers!

At first Laura's class was unruly. There were only five students. Two of them, however, were older than she was. Her days at school were not easy, but it was satisfying work.

As for living with the Bouchies, there was nothing good about it. Their house was a rundown shack. Mrs. Bouchie was cold and rude to Laura and made it clear she didn't want her there. The children misbehaved and the couple fought bitterly.

Right from the start, Laura was terribly homesick. Then, on the very first Friday, Almanzo Wilder, the town hero from the Hard Winter, showed up in a horse-drawn sleigh. He drove Laura back to De Smet for the weekend. He kept coming every weekend after that to take her home.

Laura was happy to accept rides from Almanzo. But she made it clear that he was not her boyfriend. Almanzo was ten years older than Laura. She thought of him as "Mr. Wilder." He was her father's friend. If Almanzo had other ideas, he kept them to himself—for now.

After eight weeks of teaching, Laura returned

to her own school in De Smet. Her friends were
starting to pair up, going on sleigh rides together.
Laura felt left out. So when Almanzo came
jingling up in his sleigh, Laura hopped in.

Sleigh rides turned to buggy rides in the spring.
Slowly Almanzo, quiet and steady, started to grow
on Laura.

For the next three years, Laura moved back
and forth between going to school and working.

Her weekend rides with Almanzo became longer and longer. Both of them shared a deep love of the prairie. Sometimes they rode forty miles out of town, gathering wildflowers and talking about their lives.

Almanzo had grown up on a farm in upstate New York. When he was twenty-two, he struck out for Dakota Territory to homestead. By now, he had "proved up" on his claim. That meant it was

his. Plus he owned a team of beautiful Morgans, the finest horses for miles around.

After three years of courtship, Laura and Almanzo married on August 25, 1885. He was twenty-eight; she was eighteen. Now Laura was Mrs. Wilder.

Before the wedding, Laura had the minister make her a promise. He mustn't use the standard phrase "obey your husband" in the wedding vows. Laura was staying true to her independent and strong-minded self. Fortunately, Almanzo liked her that way.

Chapter 8
Laura and Almanzo

Almanzo gave Laura a pony of her own, named Trixy. Before breakfast every morning, the newlyweds raced on horseback across the prairie. They had a house that Almanzo had built on the farm. And they owned 320 acres of good, fertile soil.

This should have been a happy and carefree time. However, their first four years together were the hardest of their lives.

Fire destroyed their new home. Hail and drought ruined their crops. Illness left Almanzo with a limp for the rest of his life.

One joy saved Laura and Almanzo from despair during those years. Their daughter, Rose, was born on December 5, 1886. Rose was a beautiful and healthy child with bright blue eyes, just like Laura's.

Laura and Almanzo had to start over. A brochure about the "Land of the Big Red Apple" advertised fruit orchards for sale in the Missouri Ozarks. Almanzo was no longer strong enough for wheat farming. A smaller farm in a warmer climate might be perfect.

In 1894, Laura set off with her family in a
covered wagon one last time. Almanzo and Laura
rode in front with Rose tucked in beside them.
The wagon carried all their belongings, including
a coop of live chickens and a lap desk that
Almanzo had made for Laura.

The Wilders rode southeast, through Nebraska and Kansas. After six weeks, they reached the hilly and rocky Missouri Ozarks. They climbed up and up, until they reached the small town of Mansfield.

On the outskirts of town, the couple bought a forty-acre farm. Laura named it Rocky Ridge. It was to be her home for the rest of her life.

ROCKY RIDGE

ALMANZO AND LAURA BUILT A ONE-OF-A-KIND HOUSE ON THEIR ROCKY RIDGE FARM. THE HOUSE TOOK THEM FIFTEEN YEARS TO COMPLETE, USING MATERIALS FROM THEIR OWN LAND. A STAIRCASE WAS SOLID OAK, MADE FROM THEIR OWN TIMBER. CHIMNEY STONES CAME FROM THE FIELDS THAT ALMANZO CLEARED. A HUGE FIREPLACE WAS MADE FROM THREE ROCKS DUG FROM THEIR GROUND.

TODAY, ROCKY RIDGE IS OPEN TO VISITORS. READERS OF THE LITTLE HOUSE BOOKS CAN SEE LAURA'S WRITING DEN UPSTAIRS AND THE DROP-LEAF DESK WHERE SHE WROTE ALL THE BOOKS.

As the years passed, the Rocky Ridge house grew bigger. More rooms were added, until there were ten. Meanwhile Laura and Almanzo were purchasing more land. They ended up with about two hundred acres.

The couple's life took on a peaceful routine that flowed from one year to the next. Laura helped Almanzo on the farm and raised a flock of chickens that were prized for their egg laying.

They were active in their community and
close to their neighbors. And each morning Laura
walked to a ridge to watch the sunrise. Nature was
still a source of wonder to her.

Rose was at school in Mansfield. A brilliant
girl, she was far ahead of her classmates. But
Rose didn't like farm work or small-town life.
She wanted a very different life from that of
her parents.

One day, when Rose was sixteen, she got her chance. Almanzo's sister, Aunt Eliza, arrived from Louisiana for a visit.

AUNT ELIZA

Rose loved her independent aunt. Aunt Eliza invited Rose to come home with her and finish high school. (Mansfield didn't have a real high school yet.) It was a hard decision.

But Laura and Almanzo agreed to let their gifted
daughter go.

The move set Rose on a very different path
from her mother's.

The opportunities that Rose found eventually
changed Laura's life, as well.

Chapter 9
Reliving Memories

By 1930, there was a famous author in the Wilder family. But it wasn't Laura; it was Rose. At the start of her career, Rose wrote for newspapers and magazines. Travel was in her blood, and Rose lived in cities on both the East and West Coasts. She also lived abroad. Rose's travels took her to France, Turkey, Albania, Egypt, and Iraq. Now and then, she returned to Rocky Ridge. But

it never suited her. Rose's far-flung way of life was highly unusual for a woman in her day—especially a woman from the rural Ozarks!

In time, Rose became a well-known novelist—Rose Wilder Lane. "Lane" was her husband's last name, and Rose kept it even though the marriage didn't last long.

Laura had begun writing herself. But her writing was part-time. She wrote for a farm paper that came out twice a month. Laura's first article was about raising chickens. She had a talent for telling stories while giving useful information. Readers liked her style so much that Laura got her own column, As a Farm Woman Thinks.

Then one day in 1930, Laura's writing took off in a whole new direction. She decided to write her autobiography. She believed that she had "stories that had to be told." Pa, Ma, and Mary had all died. And the frontier was long gone. But, in Laura's memory, these people and places were bright and alive.

Laura got out a pencil and a wide-lined school tablet. Then, sitting at her drop-leaf desk, she began writing her life story. One story after another tumbled out. She entitled the finished work "Pioneer Girl" and mailed it to Rose.

Rose passed along "Pioneer Girl" to some editors in New York. But no one was interested in a book for grown-ups about pioneer days. There already were plenty. Laura and Rose then set to work to turn Laura's memories into a picture book. Still, no one wanted to publish it—not in

that form, anyway. One editor had a suggestion, though. Why not use the stories in a book for middle-grade readers? Nothing about that time period had been written yet for them.

Laura loved the idea. Books had been so important to her at that age. And she wanted modern children to know about pioneer life— what she called "the beginning of things."

So Laura sharpened her pencils and started over. This time, instead of writing as *I*, she wrote about herself as the young girl Laura Ingalls. Her first book, *Little House in the Big Woods*, told about life in the log cabin where she was born.

Rose typed up the pages and acted as her mother's editor. In a few months, a whole book landed on the desk of a children's editor at Harper & Brothers in New York.

Getting a book published is hard for a first-time author at any time. It was especially hard in 1931 because America was in the middle of

the Great Depression. Many people didn't have enough money for clothes or food, much less books. Nonetheless, the editor liked Laura's book so much that she had to publish it. It was "the book that no depression could stop," she said later.

Little House in the Big Woods came out the next year, in 1932. Laura was sixty-five years old.

Chapter 10
The Little House Books

Reviews of Laura's first book were glowing. Fan letters from young readers meant the most to Laura, though. One girl wrote, "I wish it would never come to [an] end for it was so good."

Inspired, Laura started on a second book, called *Farmer Boy*. It told about Almanzo's childhood on his family farm in upstate New York. When that was done, she started on a third book, then a fourth . . .

Each book after *Farmer Boy* covered an entire year in Laura's life. The long journeys by covered wagon, the blizzards, grasshoppers, poverty, ruined crops: all these things came back to life in her books. As she wrote, Laura searched for exactly the right words to make scenes seem real.

It was the same thing she'd done for Mary many years before.

Laura sent her handwritten pages to Rose for editing—but not right away. "After I would write something," she said, "I would set it back for a month or so and let it cool." When she read the pages again, Laura might make a few changes before sending it to her daughter.

Rose acted as her mother's editor for all the books. She typed up the handwritten pages and returned them to Laura with tips for changes. Sometimes Rose rewrote parts herself. But she did a lot less of that as time went on and Laura became an expert writer.

Were Laura's books fiction (made-up stories) or nonfiction (all facts)? In a way, they were both. They were based on things that happened in Laura's life, and the characters and events were real. Yet she changed or omitted facts that didn't fit well into the plots. For example, her age was raised in a couple of the books. The name of the Bouchie family was changed to Brewster. The Ingallses' year in Iowa was never mentioned. Today the Little House books appear on the fiction shelf in libraries.

Laura became famous, yet her life at Rocky Ridge changed very little. Laura still did her farm chores, often in pioneer style. She churned her own butter, sewed, and canned food for the winter. But her mind often strayed to her books. Sometimes she awoke in the middle of the night with an idea. Then she'd slip out of bed and write for hours.

Laura's eighth book, *These Happy Golden Years*, was completed in 1943. The ending is her marriage to Almanzo. It was a good place to stop the series. Laura had been writing for more than ten years. Now she was seventy-six years old.

Reviewers often pointed to the themes that streamed through the books: family love, courage, independence, and cheerfulness.

Five of the Little House books became Newbery Honor titles. In publishing, that is like being nominated for an Oscar.

In 1954, the Laura Ingalls Wilder Award was created to honor children's book authors and illustrators who create important books for children. The first winner was Laura herself.

After World War II, the US government sent Laura's books to Japan and Germany, their former enemies. They thought the Ingallses represented America's pioneer spirit. It amazed Laura to receive letters from fans overseas.

Laura's books were also translated into Braille, a writing system for the blind. Her sister Mary had learned to read Braille at the Iowa College for the Blind. In her honor, Laura never accepted fees for these books.

When the series was already a best seller, Garth Williams drew new illustrations for the books.

His lifelike drawings are the ones familiar to most readers today. In 1947, Garth traveled to Rocky Ridge himself and found the eighty-year-old author and Almanzo busy in their garden. Laura's blue eyes still "sparkled with good humor," Garth said. Almanzo was leaning heavily on his cane. He didn't have long to live. Almanzo died in 1949, sixty-four years after marrying his spunky prairie sweetheart. He was ninety-two.

Laura continued to live quietly at Rocky Ridge— with a few adventures sprinkled in. At eighty-seven, she took her first airplane ride!

When she was twelve, Laura had marveled at the speed of a train—

and now this! Since her birth in a log cabin, the world had made astonishing changes. Laura had witnessed the invention of telephones, electric lights, cars, airplanes, computers, and television. Her lifelong optimism about the future had been proved right.

Laura died at home at Rocky Ridge on February 10, 1957. She was ninety years old.

Rose lived for eleven more years. In 1974, the popular TV series *Little House on the Prairie* began airing. It was loosely based on the Ingallses' real adventures.

Since Rose did not have children, her death ended the Charles Ingalls family line. Yet the Ingallses live on in the beloved Little House books.

Laura Ingalls Wilder is one of the world's most famous and loved children's authors. Today, eighty years after her first book was published, readers are still spellbound by the Ingallses' journeys across rutted prairie trails in their covered wagon.

THE LITTLE HOUSE BOOKS
BY LAURA INGALLS WILDER

LITTLE HOUSE IN THE BIG WOODS (1932)—LIFE IN PEPIN, WISCONSIN, WHERE LAURA WAS BORN

FARMER BOY (1933)—ALMANZO'S CHILDHOOD ON A FARM IN UPSTATE NEW YORK

LITTLE HOUSE ON THE PRAIRIE (1935)—LAURA'S LIFE IN INDIAN TERRITORY, KANSAS

ON THE BANKS OF PLUM CREEK (1937)—THE INGALLSES' LIFE IN WALNUT GROVE, MINNESOTA, WHERE THEY START OUT IN A SOD HOUSE

BY THE SHORES OF SILVER LAKE (1939)—LIVING AT A RAILROAD CAMP IN DAKOTA TERRITORY AND GETTING A HOMESTEAD THERE

THE LONG WINTER (1940)—SUFFERING THROUGH A BITTER WINTER IN THE FIRST YEAR OF HOMESTEADING

LITTLE TOWN ON THE PRAIRIE (1941)—THE NEW TOWN OF DE SMET SPROUTS IN THE WIDE PRAIRIE OF DAKOTA TERRITORY

THESE HAPPY GOLDEN YEARS (1943)—LAURA'S TEENAGE YEARS IN DE SMET, WHEN SHE TEACHES AND COMES TO KNOW ALMANZO

TIMELINE OF LAURA INGALLS WILDER'S LIFE

1865 — Laura's sister Mary is born in Pepin, Wisconsin

1867 — Laura Ingalls is born in Pepin, Wisconsin

1869 — The Ingallses move to Indian Territory, Kansas

1870 — Caroline Ingalls, "Carrie," is born in Kansas

1871 — The Ingallses return to the Big Woods of Wisconsin

1874 — Lives in a dugout near Walnut Grove, Minnesota

1875 — Charles Frederick Ingalls, "Freddy," is born

1876 — Laura's brother, Freddy, dies at nine months old
Laura moves with her family to Burr Oak, Iowa

1877 — Grace Ingalls is born in Burr Oak

1879 — Mary becomes blind after a fever

1880 — The Ingallses begin homesteading in De Smet,
Dakota Territory

1885 — Almanzo Wilder and Laura Ingalls marry

1886 — Rose Wilder born in De Smet

1894 — The Wilders move to Mansfield, Missouri

1932 — *Little House in the Big Woods* is published
when Laura is sixty-five

1954 — Laura awarded the first Laura Ingalls Wilder Award,
for her eight-book Little House series

1957 — Laura (age ninety) dies at her Rocky Ridge home in
Mansfield

TIMELINE OF
THE WORLD

The Homestead Act is passed, which gives land — **1862**
to settlers if they farm and live on it for five years

The Civil War ends — **1865**

The year Laura is born, the population — **1867**
of New York City is well over a million

In May, the first transcontinental railroad is completed — **1869**

The Osage people are forced to leave their homeland — **1870**
on the plains and move to a reservation in Oklahoma

Alexander Graham Bell invents the telephone — **1876**

The Great Dakota Boom begins — **1878**

Dakota Territory becomes the states — **1889**
of North Dakota and South Dakota

Ford produces the first Model T cars, which make — **1908**
automobiles affordable for many more Americans

The United States enters World War I — **1917**

The first television shows are broadcast — **1937**

The United States enters World War II after Japanese — **1941**
planes bomb Pearl Harbor on December 7

The Soviet Union launches the first satellite into space — **1957**

John F. Kennedy is elected president — **1960**

BIBLIOGRAPHY

*Anderson, William. **Laura Ingalls Wilder: A Biography**. New York: HarperCollins, 1992.

*Anderson, William. **Laura Ingalls Wilder Country: The People and Places Behind Laura Ingalls Wilder's Life and Books**. New York: HarperPerennial, 1990.

*Berne, Emma Carlson. **Laura Ingalls Wilder**. Edina, MN: ABDO Publishing Company, 2008.

*Giff, Patricia Reilly. **Laura Ingalls Wilder: Growing Up in the Little House**. New York: Viking Kestrel, 1987.

Hill, Pamela Smith. **Laura Ingalls Wilder: A Writer's Life**. Pierre: South Dakota State Historical Society Press, 2007.

Zochert, Donald. **Laura: The Life of Laura Ingalls Wilder**. Chicago: Henry Regnery Company, 1976.

*Books for young readers